JESUS

A QUICK LOOK AT THE GREATEST MAN WHO EVER LIVED

Dr. Bruce Smoll

JESUS CHRIST
A Quick Look At The
Greatest Man Who Ever Lived
By Dr. Bruce Smoll

ISBN: 979-8-9917173-8-0

All Rights Reserved. No part of this publication may be produced or transmitted in any form or by any means without written permission of the author. The author guarantees all contents are original and do not infringe upon the legal rights of any other person or work.

Prepared for Publication By

PUBLISHING

MAKING YOUR BOOK A REALITY

Cedar Point, NC | 843-929-8768 | info@BandBpublishingLLC.com

Scripture quotations marked NKJV are taken from the New King James Version®. Copyright © 1982 by Thomas Nelson. Used by permission. All rights reserved.

To contact the author: hvlm1955@gmail.com
His Victorious Life Ministry

CONTENTS

Introduction 1
JESUS CHRIST

Chapter 1 3
THE BIRTH AND EARLY YEARS OF JESUS

Chapter 2 7
THE LIFE OF JESUS

Chapter 3 15
THE MAIN TEACHINGS OF JESUS CHRIST

Chapter 4 19
UNDERSTANDING THE CONTEXT OF JESUS' LIFE

Chapter 5 33
15 PARABLES OF JESUS

Chapter 6 45
GOD CARES FOR ME!

Chapter 7 55
10 PROMISES GOD HAS MADE TO YOU

Chapter 8 63
AMAZING JESUS CHRIST FACTS

Chapter 9 71
NEXT STEPS

Introduction

JESUS CHRIST

There have been billions of people that have lived on this earth during its existence. Some have just been born and then died with little or no impact, while others have changed the world. There are many that we could name that have altered the course of history, but no one has changed the world like the man, Jesus Christ.

The book you hold in your hand is not the full presentation of His life, for that we have the greatest book ever written, the Bible. Nor is it teaching about the life of Jesus, for there are many wonderful books written by many great men and women of God that share deep insights about what the Bible says about Him. I have even written one called "***Following the Leadership and Love of Jesus***" that is available on Amazon.com. The book you hold in your hand is a quick look at the life of Jesus, His teachings, His miracles, and His legacy. It is not an exhaustive look at everything He did, but a snapshot overview for those who are beginning their walk with Him or are just curious about the Man, Jesus Christ. For the big picture view on His life I encourage you to read to books of Matthew, Mark, Luke, and John straight from the Bible.

I pray this little book is a blessing to your life and opens your eyes to receive a glimpse of the greatest man who ever lived.

Chapter 1

THE BIRTH AND EARLY YEARS OF JESUS

WHO WAS JESUS?

Jesus Christ was a Jewish man and a rabbi, born about 2,000 years ago, around 4 B.C., near Palestine. According to the Bible, Jesus is the Messiah, the Son of God, and in the Old Testament, hundreds of years before His birth, prophecies were recorded about His coming.

WHAT ABOUT HIS MOTHER?

The New Testament recounts how the angel Gabriel visited the young virgin, Mary, during her betrothal year. During this visit, Gabriel announced to her she would have a son that would be conceived by the Holy Spirit. The child she would bear would be the Messiah they had been waiting for, and He was to be named Jesus.

WHO WAS JOSEPH?

Joseph, the man Mary was engaged to, had difficulty believing what had happened, and rightfully so. Who had ever heard of a woman becoming pregnant without being with a man? He even thought of annulling the marriage, but when he was also visited by an angel in a dream, he became convinced of this miraculous event.

THE BIRTH AND EARLY YEARS OF JESUS

During that time, the Roman Empire conducted a census in the entire region, which required Jospeh and Mary to return to their hometown. Upon their return to Bethlehem, Mary was about to give birth, and no vacancies were available so, Jesus was born in a stable. Shepherds visited them, and later wise men came from the East to see the King of the Jews, as promised by the Holy Scriptures. However, when King Herod, the Roman governor of Judea, learned of the prophecy announcing the birth of the new King, he ordered all boys under the age of two to be killed.

Upon learning about Herod's intent through a dream, Joseph fled with Mary and Jesus to Egypt, where they lived until Herod died. After his death, they returned to Nazareth, a city in Galilee, where Jesus grew up and lived until the beginning of His ministry.

As a teenager, when He visited Jerusalem with His parents, He astonished the law teachers with His intelligence and deep knowledge of the Holy Scriptures.

Jesus was Jewish, both in ethnicity and nationality. Mary and Jospeh had other children, making them half brothers and sisters with Jesus (because He was conceived by the Holy Spirit). He did, however, learn Joseph's trade, carpentry. Jesus entered ministry at 30 and did not marry or have children.

Many ask whether Jesus was black or white. Jesus likely had common Middle Eastern features, with olive skin, short hair, and a beard. The Bible only says that Jesus was a man of simple appearance, as the prophecies had revealed.

Chapter 2

THE LIFE OF JESUS

THE BAPTISM AND BEGINNING OF THE MINISTRY

Jesus' baptism marks the beginning of His ministry. After being baptized in water by John the Baptist, who was His cousin and a prophet, He was led into the wilderness by the Holy Spirit. In the desert, He underwent an extreme experience, dedicating Himself to fasting and prayer for forty days, and then being tested by the devil in His knowledge of the Law and His dedication to God.

The second step at the beginning of His ministry was the selection of His disciples. Jesus handpicked 12 who would be His closest followers, whom He later designated as apostles:

Simon (Peter), Andrew, James (son of Zebedee), John, Philip, Bartholomew (Nathanael), Thomas, Matthew, James (son of Alphaeus), Thaddaeus (Judas), Simon (the Zealot), and Judas Iscariot, the betrayer.

THE MIRACLES OF JESUS

In 3 years of prophetic ministry, teaching, and preaching the Kingdom of God, Jesus performed miracles and wonders wherever He went. The first miracle of Jesus was at a wedding. According to the passage in the Gospel of John 2:1-11, He turned water into wine.

Jesus performed many other miracles. The Bible records thirty-seven. Among them are the multiplication of loaves and fishes, walking on water, many healings of paralytic, blind, and deaf people, and the resurrection of at least three who were dead.

Besides working miracles, Jesus taught, preached, and explained complex themes through parables. There are forty-four parables of Jesus in the New Testament.

THE CRUCIFIXION AND DEATH OF JESUS

With each miracle, Jesus attracted larger crowds. This bothered the religious leaders of the time, who constantly tried to conspire against His life. This finally happened when Judas Iscariot, one of Jesus' disciples, offered to hand over Him to the Pharisees in exchange for 30 pieces of silver.

During the celebration of Passover as Jesus ate with His disciples, at what we now call The Last Supper, He announced to them He would be betrayed and killed. He later went to the Mount of Olives to pray and was distressed, knowing what He was about to go through. Judas Iscariot, who had already taken the 30 pieces of silver, came to the Mount of Olives in the Garden of Gethsemane where Jesus was and betrayed Him to the authorities. Right after betraying Him, Judas was overcome with guilt and took his own life.

In that same place, the place of His betrayal, Jesus performed His last miracle before being crucified. He restored the ear of the high priest's servant, which had been cut off by Peter, one of His disciples. The Sanhedrin took and judged Jesus and then handed over to the Roman authorities. Pilate saw no reason to condemn Him, but the people preferred to release a known criminal named Barabbas and then torture and crucify Jesus on a hill called Golgotha, where criminals were executed. Before His last breath, Jesus cried out, *"My God, my God, why have you forsaken me?"*

Jesus Christ was about the age of 33-34 when He died and His body was placed in a sealed tomb with guards, so that no one could steal the body and claim He had risen from the dead.

THE RESURRECTION OF JESUS

However, even with their attempts to keep Him inside the tomb, three days after the crucifixion, Jesus Christ rose from the dead. This even came as a surprise to His closest followers. Some women who had followed His ministry and learned from His teachings went to visit His tomb but were taken aback by two angels who said that Jesus was no longer there. When the women reported the news to His disciples, they were perplexed. But their confusion was dispersed when Jesus appeared to them in the flesh! He then continued with them for 40 days and before ascending to Heaven, He gave them "The Great Commission", the mandate to spread throughout the world the message He brought, the forgiveness of sins through His death, burial, and resurrection.

THE RETURN OF JESUS

Jesus will return. The Bible records this! No one but the Father knows the hour or the day. Therefore, it is necessary to remain firm in His Word, because at the appointed time, the Shepherd will gather His sheep. Jesus will come in glory to judge humanity and establish full justice. Those who have accepted Jesus will be saved, receive eternal life, and live with Him forever!

Dr. Bruce Smoll

Chapter 3

THE MAIN TEACHINGS OF JESUS CHRIST

The four biblical books called 'the gospels' are dedicated to telling His story and His many remarkable teachings. The most famous is the Sermon on the Mount. Here are some recognizable parts:

- *'turn the other cheek'* instead of seeking revenge.

- *'go the extra mile'* when forced to walk one.

- the Lord's Prayer.

- whoever hates their neighbor is already guilty of murder.

- looking with lust at a woman is already adultery.

- love your neighbor and pray for those who persecute you.

- help, pray, and fast, without seeking visibility.

However, the essence of His teaching lies in His interpretation of the Law, declaring that the greatest commandment is to love God above all things, and your neighbor as yourself. At another time, He adds:

- This is my commandment, That ye love one another, as I have loved you.

THE LEGACY OF JESUS CHRIST

Jesus was more than a teacher, a revolutionary, or a founder of a religion. His life is exemplary and inspiring and everything He said and did brought a renewed teaching about who God really is.

The Bible declares Him as the Son of God, equal to God, who incarnated in human form to die the death of men. So, in this way, He made the path to eternal life accessible to all. He was a perfect man who was sacrificed; God raised Him from the dead and placed Him in the highest position. He is the mediator between God and men and the head of the Christian Church.

Dr. Bruce Smoll

Chapter 4

UNDERSTANDING THE CONTEXT OF JESUS' LIFE

The historical evidence states that Jesus grew up in Nazareth, a small village on top of a hill. Like every Jew of His time, He was taught by a community expert (usually in the synagogue). This education held knowledge of the Law (the books of Moses, the poetry, and the prophets), with great emphasis on the history of Israel.

These teachers could also teach reading, writing, and arithmetic. Thus, basic Jewish education formed the community in its historical and intellectual roots while providing the minimum technical skills.

The family had great importance in education since the parents' interest in the Law reflected the child's interest in the Law. It would not be wrong to assume that Jesus' parents sought to educate Him in the best way in the knowledge of the Scriptures, to where at twelve, Jesus debated at a high level with the scholars of the Temple (Luke 2:41-52).

His life, from childhood to about thirty years of age, can be summarized in these activities: study and work, for this was certainly the minimum activity a devout Jew would have. In short, Jesus was a great success in basic Jewish education for having well understood the Jewish Scriptures. His ministry, which began around the age of thirty, can be summarized by these three primary activities: teaching/preaching, healing, and exorcisms. His teachings were given through large thematic lectures, interpretation of the Law, and parables. Various groups listened: the crowd, the law teachers, and finally His disciples. The teaching method varied according to the group.

His major rivals were the Pharisees and teachers of the Law, who were the religious leaders of that time. Why were they His rivals? It certainly was not because Jesus was trying to compete and be the best, but because His life and teachings proved them as hypocritical. Their jealous hatred of Him grew to the culmination of His arrest, when He was betrayed by Judas (one of His disciples), to His sentencing, and finally to His death by the Romans.

He received the cruelest punishment of the Roman Empire, death by crucifixion. Why is it the cruelest? Because it is a very slow and torturous death and this came after already being beaten with a whip to the edge of his life and then being forced to carry His own cross.

THE RESURRECTION?

The existence of the man, Jesus, is practically no longer questioned by historians, but the big question surrounds not His life, but His resurrection. The Bible states He is the Word of God in human form, He lived a sinless life, and His death was and is a substitution for what our sinful lives deserved. When God raised Him from the dead, the Bible says we were raised with Him, the power that sin and death had over us was defeated. Jesus was the sacrifice on behalf of imperfect people, making all humanity, through faith in Him, accepted by God.

FREEDOM THROUGH TRUTH

"And ye shall know the truth, and the truth shall make you free." John 8:32 KJV

Jesus is the way, the truth, and the life. He came to free the sinner from the slavery of sin. If we allow Jesus to take the center of our lives, then we are truly transformed, and sin no longer has any power over us.

YOU WILL KNOW THE TRUTH

Many people are looking for the truth, searching for something that makes sense in their lives. From studying ancient philosophy to communicating with ChatGPT, investigating fake news, or debating the meaning of life. Throughout history, many people have tried to find out what the truth is.

In the Bible, we read that even Pilate himself asked this:

> *Pilate said to Him, "What is truth?" And when he had said this, he went out again to the Jews, and said to them, "I find no fault in Him at all. John 18:38 NKJV*

God created us to be inquisitive and ask questions, and God also provides answers to the questions we have for Him:

THE BIBLE IS THE TRUTH

Sanctify them by Your truth. Your word is truth. John 17:17 NKJV

The Bible is the revealed truth of God. When Jesus speaks to the Father in John 17:17, saying, *"Sanctify them in your truth; your word is truth,"* He is not presenting truth as something that cannot be attained, or even something deceptive. Jesus was talking about something revealed, concrete, absolute and eternal.

Today, we have access to the Bible via cell phone, computer, or tablet. We also have access to the traditional Bible, printed on paper. But we need to make the time to read the Bible and listen to its words. It's then up to us to choose how we react to the Lord's revelation. We can either accept and believe it, or we can reject it.

JESUS IS THE TRUTH

Thomas said to Him, "Lord, we do not know where You are going, and how can we know the way?" 6 Jesus said to him, "I am the way, the truth, and the life. No one comes to the Father except through Me. 7 "If you had known Me, you would have known My Father also; and from now on you know Him and have seen Him." John 14:5-7 NKJV

Not only is The Bible the truth, but Jesus Himself is the Truth. This is how He describes Himself to His disciples in John 14, and so when Jesus speaks in John 8:32, *"Then you will experience for yourselves the truth, and the truth will free you,"* He isn't presenting an abstract notion. Instead, He invites us into a transformative relationship with Himself and a journey where the truths He imparts will lead to genuine freedom.

John 14 may be the only place in the

Bible where Jesus directly says, *'I am the truth'*, but there are many passages where Jesus speaks of truth, including:

> *Pilate therefore said to Him, "Are You a king then?" Jesus answered, "You say rightly that I am a king. For this cause I was born, and for this cause I have come into the world, that I should bear witness to the truth. Everyone who is of the truth hears My voice." John 18:37 NKJV*

> *All things have been delivered to Me by My Father, and no one knows the Son except the Father. Nor does anyone know the Father except the Son, and the one to whom the Son wills to reveal Him. Matthew 11:27 NKJV*

And the truth will set you free.

> *Jesus answered them, "Most assuredly, I say to you, whoever commits sin is a slave of sin. 35 And a slave does not abide in the house forever, but a son abides forever. 36 Therefore if the Son makes you free, you shall be free indeed. John 8:34-36 NKJV*

With both Jesus and the Bible (the Word) described as truth, we see exactly how important understanding the truth is. There are plenty of passages where Jesus talks about the truth. As well as describing Himself as truth, He also refers to the message and The One (God0 who sent Him as true. You can see this in the following verses:

> *I have many things to say and*

to judge concerning you, but He who sent Me is true; and I speak to the world those things which I heard from Him. John 8:26 NKJV

Most assuredly, I say to you, he who believes in Me has everlasting life. John 6:47 NKJV

But now you seek to kill Me, a Man who has told you the truth which I heard from God. Abraham did not do this. John 8:40 NKJV

But because I tell the truth, you do not believe Me. 46 Which of you convicts Me of sin? And if I tell the truth, why do you not believe Me? 47 He who is of God hears God's words; there-

fore you do not hear, because you are not of God." John 8:45-47 NKJV

Then Jesus said to those Jews who believed Him, "If you abide in My word, you are My disciples indeed. 32 And you shall know the truth, and the truth shall make you free." John 8:31-32 NKJV

So, what does this truth provide to us? It provides us with freedom! John 8:32 makes this clear; *"and you will know the truth and the truth will set you free"*. When we know the truth, we are set free from the slavery of sin. We don't get this from philosophies, inner peace, or a concoction of other religions. Jesus is the Truth sent into the world to free it. He has been among us,

He has revealed Himself to us and He gives us access to the Father:

> *Then Jesus spoke to them again, saying, "I am the light of the world. He who follows Me shall not walk in darkness, but have the light of life." John 8:12 NKJV*

> *Stand fast therefore in the liberty by which Christ has made us free, and do not be entangled again with a yoke of bondage. Galatians 5:1 NKJV*

> *Therefore if the Son makes you free, you shall be free indeed. John 8:36 NKJV*

> *Pilate therefore said to Him, "Are You a king then?" Jesus*

answered, "You say rightly that I am a king. For this cause I was born, and for this cause I have come into the world, that I should bear witness to the truth. Everyone who is of the truth hears My voice." John 18:37 NKJV

He has delivered us from the power of darkness and conveyed us into the kingdom of the Son of His love, Colossians 1:13 NKJV

Jesus is the key that sets us free from all evil. He paid a high price to rescue us from the dominion of darkness and only Jesus can give us a transformed and free life. Let's live in this hope.

Chapter 5

15 PARABLES OF JESUS

There were many occasions when Jesus taught people using parables or short narratives. He used everyday situations people could understand to communicate the most fundamental spiritual truths.

Let us examine some of Jesus' best known parables and discover the central theme of each one.

1. THE PARABLE OF THE SOWER

The Parable of the Sower is among the most cited and shared Biblical parables and is found in Matthew 13:3-23, Mark 4:1-20, and Luke 8:4-15.

This parable presents different ways people react to the Gospel message. It shows us the importance of having a receptive heart when hearing the Word of God. When someone receives God's message with an open and prepared heart, the seed of the Word grows and produces fruit.

2. THE PARABLE OF THE GOOD SHEPHERD

In this parable found in John 10:1-18, we see Jesus as the Good Shepherd who guides and cares for His sheep. He always seeks their wellbeing. It also contrasts hired hands and thieves with Jesus. Hired hands and thieves only want to steal, kill, and destroy. But Jesus is the loving shepherd willing to give His life for His sheep.

3. THE PARABLE OF THE GOOD SAMARITAN

Found in Luke 10:25-37, the central

theme of this parable is that God's love in our hearts overcomes all prejudice and moves us to action.

Jesus uses the parable to answer the question from an expert in the law who asks, 'Who is my neighbor?' - It presents a man injured on the road and the reactions of those passing by. The least expected person was the one who showed compassion to the injured man. Jesus calls us to live lives full of love for our 'neighbors' and compassion in response to the needs of those around us.

4. THE PARABLE OF THE WHEAT AND THE WEEDS

This parable, found in Matthew 13:24-30, speaks about the reality we live in. The coexistence of wheat and the weed in the story illustrates the reality of good and evil existing together in the world until the end of time. However, at the end of time, the groups will be separated, and each will go to their eternal destiny.

5. THE PARABLE OF THE PRODIGAL SON

This parable speaks about God's immense love for each human being. Found in Luke 15:11-32, we learn that no matter how far we have strayed from our Heavenly Father; He is there with open arms, ready to receive us. He always forgives those who come to Him with a repentant heart.

6. THE PARABLE OF THE MUSTARD SEED

This short parable appears in three of the Gospels: Matthew 13:31-32, Mark 4:30-32, and Luke 13:18-19. With it, we learn that when the kingdom of God enters a person's heart; it is like a small seed. With proper care, that seed will grow and become a large tree. That strong and leafy tree will serve as support and rest for all who come near it.

7. THE PARABLE OF THE RICH MAN AND LAZARUS

The parable found in Luke 16:19-31 speaks of two men. One was a rich man who lived surrounded by luxuries. The other was a beggar covered with sores who sat at the entrance of the rich man's house, desiring to eat at least the crumbs left by the other.

Both men died, and the parable tells us that the rich man went to Hades and the poor man to Abraham's side. The parable continues to emphasize that each person will have an eternal destiny. The two options are Abraham's side (paradise) or Hell (place of torment). That destiny is decided while we are alive, based on our response to God's Word.

8. THE PARABLE OF THE YEAST

This parable can be read in Matthew 13:33 and Luke 13:20-21. It gives a glimpse into what the Kingdom of Heaven is like. It is compared to yeast that arrives, spreads, and encompasses everything. Therefore, the kingdom of God has the power to transform people and continually grow.

9. THE PARABLE OF THE PHARISEE AND THE TAX COLLECTOR

In this parable, Jesus told the story of two men: a Pharisee and a tax collector. The text of the parable is found in Luke 18:9-14.

One day, these two men went to the temple to pray. The Pharisees spoke proudly before God and thanked Him for not being as sinful as other people. However, the tax collector approached God with humility and pleaded for the Father's mercy. Jesus affirmed it was the tax collector who received God's mercy and forgiveness.

With this parable, we learn that we should have humble hearts before God, not elevating ourselves above others, and recognizing our need for Him. God exalts the humble and humbles the proud.

10. THE PARABLE OF THE HIDDEN TREASURE

Another short parable that occupies a single verse is found in Matthew 13:44. It speaks of the Kingdom of Heaven as the greatest treasure we could ever have. There is and never will be anything more valuable than eternal life with God! Upon finding this treasure, everything else becomes secondary.

11. THE PARABLE OF THE PERSISTENT WIDOW AND THE UNJUST JUDGE

This parable, which we can read in Luke 18:1-8, is about persevering in prayer. It presents an unjust and insensitive judge and a widow who would not give up. The judge, although he had no fear of God, delivered justice and answered the widow's petition. Similarly, we must persistently bring our requests before God without growing weary.

12. THE PARABLE OF THE WISE AND FOOLISH BUILDERS

The central theme of this parable is the importance not only of hearing God's Word but also obeying it. By doing so, we stand on the Rock, and though we may still go through storms in life, they will not destroy us. We can read the parable in Matthew 7:24-27 and Luke 6:46-49. If we live a life of obedience to God, we will stand firm against the problems and difficulties that life brings.

13. THE PARABLE OF THE TEN VIRGINS

This parable speaks about ten virgins waiting for the bridegroom. We can read it in Matthew 25:1-13. Five of the virgins were wise and brought extra oil. The other five did not. The bridegroom was delayed, and only the wise were prepared to receive him.

We need to follow the example of the five wise virgins and be prepared for the second coming of the Lord Jesus Christ, since we do not know the day or the hour He will return.

14. THE PARABLE OF THE SHEEP AND THE GOATS

Matthew 25:31-46 presents a very important but challenging parable. It is a prophetic message about how God will judge the nations. In this parable, Jesus describes the Son of Man coming in glory, accompanied by angels, to sit on His throne. Nations gather before Him, and He separates people as a shepherd separates sheep from goats.

The sheep representing the righteous are commended for their acts of kindness, such as feeding the hungry, giving drink to the thirsty, welcoming strangers, clothing the naked, and visiting the sick and imprisoned. The righteous are surprised and ask when they did these acts, to which He responds, "Truly I tell you, whatever you did for one of the least of these brothers and sisters of mine, you did for Me."

The parable then shares a warning of 'eternal punishment' to those who saw people in need and did nothing to help them, and with that, it emphasizes the importance of helping others because, by serving them, we serve the Lord.

15. THE PARABLE OF THE NET

The text of this parable is in Matthew 13:47-50. In this story, Jesus compares the kingdom of heaven to a net that catches fish of every kind. When the net is full, the fishermen separate the good fish from the bad. The good fish are kept, while the bad ones are thrown out.

The parable tells us that in this world, Christians and non-Christians coexist. The message of salvation (or the net) is thrown to all, but not all accept it. At the end of time, there will be a final judgment where the righteous and the wicked will be separated. Those who accepted the message of salvation will go to one place, and those who did not will go to another.

Chapter 6

GOD CARES FOR ME!

Life sometimes gives us difficult moments when we feel weak, afraid, lonely, or uncertain along the way, but we must not forget how great God's love is for us. When the struggles seem stronger, don't be discouraged: God cares for you!

He is the light at the end of the dark tunnel of your suffering and He wants to help you see a new life, full of peace and victory. Take a look at these seven Bible verses that talk about how God takes care of us down to the smallest detail:

1. GOD KNOWS AND CARES FOR ALL CREATURES

He causes the grass to grow for the cattle, and vegetation for the service of man, that he may bring forth food from the earth, 15 And wine that makes glad the heart of man, oil to make his face shine, and bread which strengthens man's heart. Psalm 104:14-15 NKJV

As well as being Creator, God is the preserver of all things. He continues to cherish creation with goodness and mercy. He knows and cares for all creatures (Psalm 145:9). Because of Him, the world still stands today. God continually extends His care to the natural world so that life can continue its course on earth until the end. Be grateful for God's kind care for all creation!

2. GOD PLACES HIGH VALUE ON YOU.

Are not two sparrows sold for a copper coin? And not one of them falls to the ground apart from your Father's will. 30 But the very hairs of your head are all numbered. 31 Do not fear therefore; you are of more value than many sparrows. Matthew 10:29-31 NKJV

God oversees the entire universe, but not only that, He governs and preserves all things, even the smallest detail, with His care and love. He does this so that all things fulfill the purpose for which they were created. So, know that you have a special purpose, and God will take care of your life until all the plans He has for you are fulfilled. Never forget you were made to glorify God!

3. GOD CARES FOR THOSE WHO LOVE HIM

The Lord is near to all who call upon Him, to all who call upon Him in truth. 19 He will fulfill the desire of those who fear Him; He also will hear their cry and save them. 20 The Lord preserves all who love Him, but all the wicked He will destroy. Psalm 145:18-20 NKJV

God sustains the entire universe, but He has a special care for His people all over the world. These people possess something characteristic of God Himself: Love. God loves His people and cares for them. He cares for those who love Him with all their hearts. Even if you are going through difficulties, you can believe and trust in Christ!

He tells you to take heart (John 16:33)!

> *These things I have spoken to you, that in Me you may have peace. In the world you will have tribulation; but be of good cheer, I have overcome the world." John 16:33 NKJV*

In Jesus' presence, there is always peace, joy, and hope, even when there are difficulties. He can deliver from all dangers those who truly trust in His love and grace.

4. GOD SAYS NOT TO FEAR

Do not fear, little flock, for it is your Father's good pleasure to give you the kingdom. Luke 12:32 NKJV

Total and sincere trust in God's care is one characteristic of the Lord's children. Like the Good Shepherd, He takes care of all His sheep; nothing you need will be lacking (Psalm 23). With this in mind, don't be afraid of the difficulties that may arise. Trust in the Love that sustains you every day. Remember that life is not just about this time here in the world, but it continues and goes on to eternity in the Kingdom of God. Be confident, because God has promised to give us a place with Him in that glorious Kingdom!

5. GOD PROTECTS AND SUSTAINS

"You have hedged me behind and before, and laid Your hand upon me." Psalm 139:5 NKJV

God preserves and governs all things; He surrounds us with His divine protection and love. Greater than any bodyguard, God delivers us from evils we are unaware of. He leads the way and lays His hand on you as a covering. Even if there are threats and dangers outside, remember that God is the Father who protects you every day of your life. Pray and be grateful for the caring love of the Lord of Life.

6. GOD COMFORTS IN THE MIDST OF PAIN

Blessed are the peacemakers: for they shall be called the children of God. Matthew 5:9 KJV

In the dark times of the soul, know that God does not despise the tears of those who suffer. He comforts the wounded heart that turns to Him in prayer. Like a small child who seeks comfort in the arms of his parents, cling to your heavenly Father's hands right now and seek His help! He sees your tears and can comfort you... Even if you do not understand why certain things happen, put your hope and trust in God. He cares for you!

7. GOD IS PRESENT!

They shall not hunger nor thirst; neither shall the heat nor sun smite them: for he that hath mercy on them shall lead them, even by the springs of water shall he guide them. Isaiah 49:10 KJV

Fear thou not; for I am with thee: be not dismayed; for I am thy God: I will strengthen thee; yea, I will help thee; yea, I will uphold thee with the right hand of my righteousness. Isaiah 41:10 KJV

Remember when you were a child, and you were afraid of the dark? You certainly felt safer and more confident when you had someone brave (an adult) by your side, didn't you? It is the same with us and God. Even though we are "grown-up", we are like children to our heavenly Father. When fear comes to haunt you, when there's terrible news and threats, remember that you are not alone in this world. God is watching over your life, and not from a distance... He is present! Even now, He is holding you with His mighty hands. Remember that He is watching over you!

God is just a prayer away. Cry out to the Lord with sincerity, faith, and love. He will come to your aid and help you overcome your needs. You are not alone in times of suffering and storm.

Chapter 7

10 PROMISES GOD HAS MADE TO YOU

God has promised you many good things! Life is not always easy, but God has good plans for you. He desires your well-being and happiness, and promises these 10 things:

1. SALVATION

And this is the promise that He has promised us—eternal life.
1 John 2:25 NKJV

If you have repented and accepted Jesus as your Savior, you have eternal life. Heaven is your great hope! Never forget that.

2. ABUNDANT LIFE

The thief does not come except to steal, and to kill, and to destroy. I have come that they may have life, and that they may have it more abundantly. John 10:10 NKJV

God does not promise an easy life, but He promises a good life. He has the power to restore what the enemy has stolen, resurrect what has died, and rebuild what has been destroyed.

3. THE HOLY SPIRIT

If you then, being evil, know how to give good gifts to your children, how much more will your heavenly Father give the Holy Spirit to those who ask Him! Luke 11:13 NKJV

The very power that Jesus had to accomplish all that He accomplished in life is now available to everyone who follows Jesus Christ. All we need to do is ask!

4. PEACE

These things I have spoken to you, that in Me you may have peace. In the world you will have tribulation; but be of good cheer, I have overcome the world." John 16:33 NKJV

God's peace helps to overcome all difficulties. God will never abandon you. He is always with you to give you peace when you need it most.

5. DAILY PROVISION

"Therefore do not worry, saying, 'What shall we eat?' or

'What shall we drink?' or 'What shall we wear?' 32 For after all these things the Gentiles seek. For your heavenly Father knows that you need all these things. 33 But seek first the kingdom of God and His righteousness, and all these things shall be added to you. Matthew 6:31-33 NKJV

God cares about every aspect of your life. When you live to please Him, He takes care of your needs. You may not be rich, but God will provide what you need at the right time.

6. PROTECTION

No evil shall befall you, nor shall any plague come near your dwelling; Psalm 91:10 NKJV

Despite challenges and struggles, God protects us from evil and disaster. Those who believe in God receive the promise of His protection. Trust in Him!

7. WISDOM

If any of you lacks wisdom, let him ask of God, who gives to all liberally and without reproach, and it will be given to him. James 1:5 NKJV

God is the source of all wisdom, and if we need wisdom, all we need to do is recognize our need, ask Him for it, and then we can expect Him to give us the wisdom we need. It may come through reading the Bible, God may speak personally to our hearts, or He may even use another person to share it with us.

8. PROSPERITY

For I know the thoughts that I think toward you, says the Lord, thoughts of peace and not of evil, to give you a future and a hope. Jeremiah 29:11 NKJV

We must remember that prosperity involves more than just material possessions. A prosperous life is a life where God is blessing every aspect of our life. This is His desire and end goal. All we need to do is align ourselves with His plan.

9. NEW HEART

I will give you a new heart and put a new spirit within you; I will take the heart of stone out of your flesh and give you a heart of flesh. Ezekiel 36:26 NKJV

God wants to renew our minds and give us a new heart. A heart free from hurt, bitterness, and malice. A moldable, lovable, and obedient heart to Him.

10. HE IS FAITHFUL TO FULFILL HIS PROMISES!

My covenant I will not break, nor alter the word that has gone out of My lips. Psalm 89:34 NKJV

God fulfills His promises; unlike man, He does not lie. For God, everything is possible; there is no promise too difficult to fulfill. What God promised will be fulfilled because His word does not change.

Dr. Bruce Smoll

Chapter 8

AMAZING JESUS CHRIST FACTS

- Nearly all scholars (Biblical and secular) agree that Jesus Christ existed. However, they don't agree on how well the Jesus in the Bible accurately reflects Jesus as a historical figure.

- Contrary to what Christians believe, most Jews believe that Jesus Christ was not the Messiah and did not fulfill the Messianic prophecy. They also do not believe that Christ was resurrected or divine.

- At the time of Jesus' birth, the town of Nazareth only had about 200–400 people. In the New Testament, the town is a literal joke, as seen in the Bible when someone says, "Can anything good come out of Nazareth?"

- Jesus worked as a carpenter, possibly from ages 12 to 30, which means for roughly 18 years, Jesus was akin to a day laborer.

- Even Jesus needed "alone time." The Gospels frequently mention that Jesus needed to withdraw from the crowds. One cave where He spent some time is called the Eremos Cave, from which the words "desolate" and "hermit" derive.

- Some scholars note Jesus did not want to die. In the Garden of Gethsemane, He says, "Remove this cup from Me" (Luke 22:42) and "My soul is sorrowful even unto death." (Matthew 26:38).

- Some of Jesus' critics in the Bible accuse Him of drinking too much wine (Matthew 11:1 The Son of man came eating and drinking, and they say, Behold a man gluttonous, and a winebibber, a friend of publicans and sinners. But wisdom is justified of her children.)

- During His life, Jesus was considered to be a radical because He talked to women, spent time with sinners, and allowed His followers to pick grain on the Sabbath.

- Because Jesus was a Jew, He almost certainly had Jewish features, such as olive skin, brown eyes, and dark hair.

- Scholars believe Jesus was about

5 feet, 5 inches (1.7 meters) tall, which is about the average height for an adult male during that time period.

- During the time of Christ, most Jews used only one name, which could be followed either by the phrase "son of . . . " or the person's hometown, which is why Jesus is often referred to as Jesus of Nazareth.

- Scholars note that there were two solar eclipses around the time of Jesus' death: one in 29 AD, and one in 33 AD. The Christian Gospels state the skies darkened after the crucifixion, which suggests that His death coincided with one of these eclipses.

- The Sanhedrin arrested and tried Jesus Christ. Pontius Pilate sentenced Him to be scourged and crucified.

- Before Jesus died, He said, "I am thirsty." In response, He was offered wine mixed with myrrh or gall to drink. He refused it.

- According to the gospels of Mark and John, Jesus appeared first to Mary Magdalene after His resurrection. She was involved in His ministry from the beginning to His death, and she is mentioned more times than most of the apostles.

- Mary Magdalene initially mistook Jesus for the gardener until He said her name.

- It took Jesus six hours to die after He was hung on the cross.

- Torture in Christ's day was meant to psychologically destroy someone before they died from any physical wounds.

- While most scholars agree that Christ's crucifixion is an indisputable fact, they disagree about the reasons and context for it.

- The path that Jesus took to His crucifixion is called the "Via Dolorosa," which is Latin for "Way of Grief" or "Way of Suffering."

- Because the Romans felt like it was too gruesome to crucify someone in town, they made people carry their cross to the outskirts of town, which, in Christ's case, was to Golgotha.

- The word "crucifixion," literally means "fixed to a cross."

- The Roman orator Cicero noted that, of all the punishments, *"cru-*

cifixion is the cruelest and most terrifying."

- "Christ" is a title that comes from a Greek word meaning "Anointed One."

- While hanging on the cross, Jesus told one of His disciples to take care of Mary, His mother.

- The word "halo", is from the Greek word "halos," or "disk of the sun or moon, ring of light around the sun or moon"

- The halo that often adorns Christ's and other saints' heads in works of art was originally a feature of the sun god (Apollo or Sol Invictus). It was appropriated for images of Christ to show His heavenly power.

- According to many scholars, Joseph, the man who raised Jesus, died by the time Jesus started His ministry. This is perhaps why Jesus is often referred to as Jesus, the son of Mary.

- After Jesus' death, His brother James became a leader of the Jerusalem church.

- The Shroud of Turin is the best known relic of Jesus and one of the most studied objects in human history.

Chapter 9

NEXT STEPS

You may have arrived at the end of this book and realized that you have never made a commitment to Jesus, maing Him the Lord of your life. But how, how does this work? How can we make Jesus the Lord of your life and be restored back to God through Him? The answer to this is very simple. It is as simple as ABC.

1. ADMIT

First, we must admit that by our very nature; we are sinners. Sin entered this world when Adam, the first man, listened to what the devil said, instead of obeying what God has spoken to him.

> *Therefore, just as through one man, sin entered the world, and death through sin, and thus death spread to all men, because all sinned. Romans 5:12 NKJV*

We also admit that there is nothing we can do to fix ourselves. We need a Savior to free us from our sin.

2. BELIEVE

We believe Jesus died on the cross for the payment of our sins and then three days later, God raised Him from the dead.

> *"Therefore, as through one man's offense, judgment came to all men, resulting in condemnation, even so, through one man's righteous act the free gift came to all men, re-*

sulting in justification of life. 19 For as by one man's disobedience many were made sinners, so also by one Man's obedience many will be made righteous." Romans 5:18-19 NKJV

"And He Himself is the propitiation for our sins, and not for ours only but also for the whole world." 1 John 2:2 NKJV

3. CONFESS

We confess that Jesus Christ is the Lord and Savior of our life. Accepting what Jesus did on the cross is so much more than just a one-way ticket to Heaven when we die. It is a complete restoration to what God intended for man to be. Our model and example is Jesus Christ. That is why He must be the Lord of our life. We look to Him and the life He lived to give us direction and guidance.

> *"That if you confess with your mouth, the Lord Jesus and believe in your heart that God has raised Him from the dead, you will be saved. 10 For with the heart one believes unto righteousness, and with the mouth confession is made unto salvation." Romans 10:9-10 NKJV*

If you know you need Jesus because of the sin problem in your life, you can pray this prayer now.

"Lord Jesus, I know and admit openly I am a sinner. I believe You died for my sins and rose from the dead. I choose today to turn from my sins and invite

you to come into my heart and life. I now, by the grace of God, choose to trust and follow Your leading in my life as I confess You as my Lord and Savior. In Jesus' Name. Amen."

If you prayed this prayer of salvation and commitment to Jesus, I now encourage you to find a Bible believing church to attend and learn more about what God says in His Word.

Made in the USA
Columbia, SC
03 June 2025